Families

Around the World

Clare Lewis

Edited by Joanna Issa, Shelly Lyons, Diyan Leake and Helen Cox Cannons
Designed by Cynthia Akiyoshi
Original illustrations © Capstone Global Library Ltd 2014
Picture research by Elizabeth Alexander and Tracy Cummins
Production by Victoria Fitzgerald
Originated by Capstone Global Library Ltd
Printed and bound in China

ISBN 978 1 406 28199 6
18 17 16 15 14
10 9 8 7 6 5 4 3 2 1

British Library Cataloguing in Publication Data

A full catalogue record for this book is available from the British Library.

Acknowledgements

We would like to thank the following for permission to reproduce photographs: Alamy pp. 4 & 22e (both © Gavin Hellier), 8 & 22d (both © Jake Lyell), 18 (© IndiaPicture), 19 & 22c (both © Paul Springett 06), 21 (© Design Pics Inc.), 23 (© IndiaPicture); Corbis p. 13 (© Hill Street Studios/Blend Images); Getty Images pp. 4, 20 & 22a (all Wayne R Bilenduke), 7 (Hero Images), 9 (Ariel Skelley), 11 (Todd Wright), 17 (Tom Merton); Shutterstock pp. 1 & 2 (both © iofoto), 5 & 15 (both © Monkey Business Images), 10 (© Andy Dean Photography), 12 (© Nolte Lourens), 16 & 23 (both © spotmatik); Superstock pp. 6 (Blend Images), 14 & 22b (both Stock Connection).

Cover photograph of a playful family in front of their house reproduced with permission of SuperStock (Corbis). Back cover photograph reproduced with permission of Shutterstock (© Monkey Business Images).

Every effort has been made to contact copyright holders of material reproduced in this book. Any omissions will be rectified in subsequent printings if notice is given to the publisher.

All the internet addresses (URLs) given in this book were valid at the time of going to press. However, due to the dynamic nature of the Internet, some addresses may have changed, or sites may have changed or ceased to exist since publication. While the author and publisher regret any inconvenience this may cause readers, no responsibility for any such changes can be accepted by either the author or the publisher.

Contents

Families everywhere

Families live all over the world.
Every family is different.

parents

grandparents

children

A family is a group of people who are related to each other.

Different types of families

Some families are big.

Some families are small.

Some families live together.

Some families live far apart.

Sometimes people in a family look
a bit like each other.

Sometimes two families join
together to make one family.

What do families do?

Families look after each other.

Families help each other.

Some families work together.

Some families play together.

Some families exercise together.

Some families look after pets together.

Some families celebrate festivals together.

Some families travel together.

Families are everywhere.

Who is in your family?

Map of families around the world

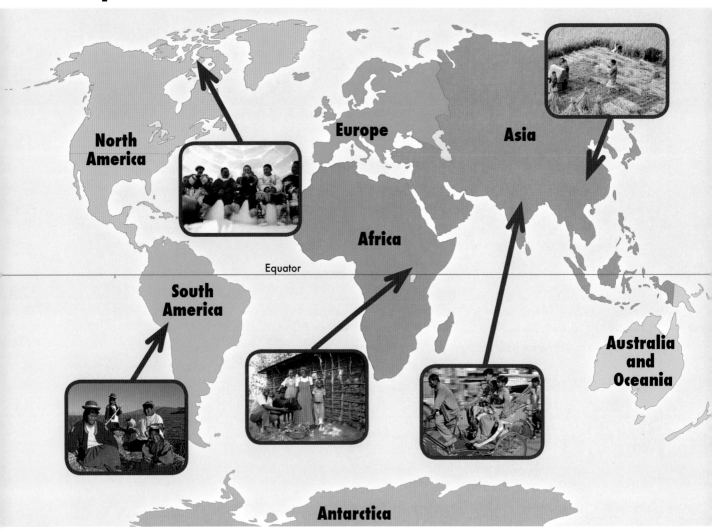

North America

Europe

Asia

Africa

Equator

South America

Australia and Oceania

Antarctica

Picture glossary

exercise do an activity that helps you stay healthy

festival special time for a group of people

Index

Notes for parents and teachers

Before reading

Show children the cover of the book and read the title. Then turn to the contents page. With the children, read the entries on the contents page and explain that this is a tool to help readers know what information is in the book and where to find it. Ask children to predict what they will learn from this book after reading the table of contents.

After reading

- Turn to page 5 and discuss how labels are used with the picture to identify different members of the family. Have children name other types of family members (aunt, uncle, cousin, etc.). Then, have them draw a picture of their own family and label the family members.

- Discuss how this book has examples of families from all over the world. Discuss how there are many similarities with families, no matter where they live. Have children look at the photo on page 4. Then, point out the map on page 22. Demonstrate for children how to use the map to identify that the photo on page 4 was taken in South America.

Note on picture on page 19 & 22: NEVER ride a bicycle without a helmet.